Stock Exchange Trader's Portfolio

JAMES F. HATCHER III

ISBN-13: 978-1981764785
ISBN-10: 198176478X

Available from Amazon.com, CreateSpace.com,
and other retail outlets.

Published by The Masonic Press.
Find more interesting titles on our website:

masonicpress.com

Printed by CreateSpace, Charleston, SC
An Amazon.com Company

SYMBOL:_____ Exchange:_____

DATE	BUY @ PRICE	BUY AMOUNT	MIN SELL PT	SELL @ PRICE	SELL AMOUNT	PROFIT/LOSS

SYMBOL:_____ Exchange:_____

DATE	BUY @ PRICE	BUY AMOUNT	MIN SELL PT	SELL @ PRICE	SELL AMOUNT	PROFIT/LOSS

SYMBOL:_____ Exchange:_____

DATE	BUY @ PRICE	BUY AMOUNT	MIN SELL PT	SELL @ PRICE	SELL AMOUNT	PROFIT/LOSS

SYMBOL:_____ Exchange:_____

DATE	BUY @ PRICE	BUY AMOUNT	MIN SELL PT	SELL @ PRICE	SELL AMOUNT	PROFIT/LOSS

SYMBOL:_____ Exchange:_____

DATE	BUY @ PRICE	BUY AMOUNT	MIN SELL PT	SELL @ PRICE	SELL AMOUNT	PROFIT/LOSS

SYMBOL:_____ Exchange:_____

DATE	BUY @ PRICE	BUY AMOUNT	MIN SELL PT	SELL @ PRICE	SELL AMOUNT	PROFIT/LOSS

SYMBOL:_____ Exchange:_____

DATE	BUY @ PRICE	BUY AMOUNT	MIN SELL PT	SELL @ PRICE	SELL AMOUNT	PROFIT/LOSS

SYMBOL:_____ Exchange:_____

DATE	BUY @ PRICE	BUY AMOUNT	MIN SELL PT	SELL @ PRICE	SELL AMOUNT	PROFIT/LOSS

SYMBOL:_____ Exchange:_____

DATE	BUY @ PRICE	BUY AMOUNT	MIN SELL PT	SELL @ PRICE	SELL AMOUNT	PROFIT/LOSS

SYMBOL:_____ Exchange:_____

DATE	BUY @ PRICE	BUY AMOUNT	MIN SELL PT	SELL @ PRICE	SELL AMOUNT	PROFIT/LOSS

SYMBOL:_____ Exchange:_____

DATE	BUY @ PRICE	BUY AMOUNT	MIN SELL PT	SELL @ PRICE	SELL AMOUNT	PROFIT/LOSS

SYMBOL:_____ Exchange:_____

DATE	BUY @ PRICE	BUY AMOUNT	MIN SELL PT	SELL @ PRICE	SELL AMOUNT	PROFIT/LOSS

SYMBOL:_____ Exchange:_____

DATE	BUY @ PRICE	BUY AMOUNT	MIN SELL PT	SELL @ PRICE	SELL AMOUNT	PROFIT/LOSS

SYMBOL:_____ Exchange:_____

DATE	BUY @ PRICE	BUY AMOUNT	MIN SELL PT	SELL @ PRICE	SELL AMOUNT	PROFIT/LOSS

SYMBOL:_____ Exchange:_____

DATE	BUY @ PRICE	BUY AMOUNT	MIN SELL PT	SELL @ PRICE	SELL AMOUNT	PROFIT/LOSS

SYMBOL:_____ Exchange:_____

DATE	BUY @ PRICE	BUY AMOUNT	MIN SELL PT	SELL @ PRICE	SELL AMOUNT	PROFIT/LOSS

SYMBOL:_____ Exchange:_____

DATE	BUY @ PRICE	BUY AMOUNT	MIN SELL PT	SELL @ PRICE	SELL AMOUNT	PROFIT/LOSS

SYMBOL:_____ Exchange:_____

DATE	BUY @ PRICE	BUY AMOUNT	MIN SELL PT	SELL @ PRICE	SELL AMOUNT	PROFIT/LOSS

SYMBOL:_____ Exchange:_____

DATE	BUY @ PRICE	BUY AMOUNT	MIN SELL PT	SELL @ PRICE	SELL AMOUNT	PROFIT/LOSS

SYMBOL:_____ Exchange:_____

DATE	BUY @ PRICE	BUY AMOUNT	MIN SELL PT	SELL @ PRICE	SELL AMOUNT	PROFIT/LOSS

SYMBOL:_____ Exchange:_____

DATE	BUY @ PRICE	BUY AMOUNT	MIN SELL PT	SELL @ PRICE	SELL AMOUNT	PROFIT/LOSS

SYMBOL:_____ Exchange:_____

DATE	BUY @ PRICE	BUY AMOUNT	MIN SELL PT	SELL @ PRICE	SELL AMOUNT	PROFIT/LOSS

SYMBOL:_____ Exchange:_____

DATE	BUY @ PRICE	BUY AMOUNT	MIN SELL PT	SELL @ PRICE	SELL AMOUNT	PROFIT/LOSS

SYMBOL:_____ Exchange:_____

DATE	BUY @ PRICE	BUY AMOUNT	MIN SELL PT	SELL @ PRICE	SELL AMOUNT	PROFIT/LOSS

SYMBOL:_____ Exchange:_____

DATE	BUY @ PRICE	BUY AMOUNT	MIN SELL PT	SELL @ PRICE	SELL AMOUNT	PROFIT/LOSS

SYMBOL:_____ Exchange:_____

DATE	BUY @ PRICE	BUY AMOUNT	MIN SELL PT	SELL @ PRICE	SELL AMOUNT	PROFIT/LOSS

SYMBOL:_____ Exchange:_____

DATE	BUY @ PRICE	BUY AMOUNT	MIN SELL PT	SELL @ PRICE	SELL AMOUNT	PROFIT/LOSS

SYMBOL:_____ Exchange:_____

DATE	BUY @ PRICE	BUY AMOUNT	MIN SELL PT	SELL @ PRICE	SELL AMOUNT	PROFIT/LOSS

SYMBOL:_____ Exchange:_____

DATE	BUY @ PRICE	BUY AMOUNT	MIN SELL PT	SELL @ PRICE	SELL AMOUNT	PROFIT/LOSS

SYMBOL:_____ Exchange:_____

DATE	BUY @ PRICE	BUY AMOUNT	MIN SELL PT	SELL @ PRICE	SELL AMOUNT	PROFIT/LOSS

SYMBOL:_____ Exchange:_____

DATE	BUY @ PRICE	BUY AMOUNT	MIN SELL PT	SELL @ PRICE	SELL AMOUNT	PROFIT/LOSS

SYMBOL:_____ Exchange:_____

DATE	BUY @ PRICE	BUY AMOUNT	MIN SELL PT	SELL @ PRICE	SELL AMOUNT	PROFIT/LOSS

SYMBOL:_____ Exchange:_____

DATE	BUY @ PRICE	BUY AMOUNT	MIN SELL PT	SELL @ PRICE	SELL AMOUNT	PROFIT/LOSS

SYMBOL:_____ Exchange:_____

DATE	BUY @ PRICE	BUY AMOUNT	MIN SELL PT	SELL @ PRICE	SELL AMOUNT	PROFIT/LOSS

SYMBOL:_____ Exchange:_____

DATE	BUY @ PRICE	BUY AMOUNT	MIN SELL PT	SELL @ PRICE	SELL AMOUNT	PROFIT/LOSS

SYMBOL:_____ Exchange:_____

DATE	BUY @ PRICE	BUY AMOUNT	MIN SELL PT	SELL @ PRICE	SELL AMOUNT	PROFIT/LOSS

SYMBOL:_____ Exchange:_____

DATE	BUY @ PRICE	BUY AMOUNT	MIN SELL PT	SELL @ PRICE	SELL AMOUNT	PROFIT/LOSS

SYMBOL:_____ Exchange:_____

DATE	BUY @ PRICE	BUY AMOUNT	MIN SELL PT	SELL @ PRICE	SELL AMOUNT	PROFIT/LOSS

SYMBOL:_____ Exchange:_____

DATE	BUY @ PRICE	BUY AMOUNT	MIN SELL PT	SELL @ PRICE	SELL AMOUNT	PROFIT/LOSS

SYMBOL:_____ Exchange:_____

DATE	BUY @ PRICE	BUY AMOUNT	MIN SELL PT	SELL @ PRICE	SELL AMOUNT	PROFIT/LOSS

SYMBOL:_____ Exchange:_____

DATE	BUY @ PRICE	BUY AMOUNT	MIN SELL PT	SELL @ PRICE	SELL AMOUNT	PROFIT/LOSS

SYMBOL:_____ Exchange:_____

DATE	BUY @ PRICE	BUY AMOUNT	MIN SELL PT	SELL @ PRICE	SELL AMOUNT	PROFIT/LOSS

SYMBOL:_____ Exchange:_____

DATE	BUY @ PRICE	BUY AMOUNT	MIN SELL PT	SELL @ PRICE	SELL AMOUNT	PROFIT/LOSS

SYMBOL:_____ Exchange:_____

DATE	BUY @ PRICE	BUY AMOUNT	MIN SELL PT	SELL @ PRICE	SELL AMOUNT	PROFIT/LOSS

SYMBOL:_____ Exchange:_____

DATE	BUY @ PRICE	BUY AMOUNT	MIN SELL PT	SELL @ PRICE	SELL AMOUNT	PROFIT/LOSS

SYMBOL:_____ Exchange:_____

DATE	BUY @ PRICE	BUY AMOUNT	MIN SELL PT	SELL @ PRICE	SELL AMOUNT	PROFIT/LOSS

SYMBOL:_____ Exchange:_____

DATE	BUY @ PRICE	BUY AMOUNT	MIN SELL PT	SELL @ PRICE	SELL AMOUNT	PROFIT/LOSS

SYMBOL:_____ Exchange:_____

DATE	BUY @ PRICE	BUY AMOUNT	MIN SELL PT	SELL @ PRICE	SELL AMOUNT	PROFIT/LOSS

SYMBOL:_____ Exchange:_____

DATE	BUY @ PRICE	BUY AMOUNT	MIN SELL PT	SELL @ PRICE	SELL AMOUNT	PROFIT/LOSS

SYMBOL:_____ Exchange:_____

DATE	BUY @ PRICE	BUY AMOUNT	MIN SELL PT	SELL @ PRICE	SELL AMOUNT	PROFIT/LOSS

SYMBOL:_____ Exchange:_____

DATE	BUY @ PRICE	BUY AMOUNT	MIN SELL PT	SELL @ PRICE	SELL AMOUNT	PROFIT/LOSS

SYMBOL:_____ Exchange:_____

DATE	BUY @ PRICE	BUY AMOUNT	MIN SELL PT	SELL @ PRICE	SELL AMOUNT	PROFIT/LOSS

SYMBOL:_____ Exchange:_____

DATE	BUY @ PRICE	BUY AMOUNT	MIN SELL PT	SELL @ PRICE	SELL AMOUNT	PROFIT/LOSS

SYMBOL:_____ Exchange:_____

DATE	BUY @ PRICE	BUY AMOUNT	MIN SELL PT	SELL @ PRICE	SELL AMOUNT	PROFIT/LOSS

SYMBOL:_____ Exchange:_____

DATE	BUY @ PRICE	BUY AMOUNT	MIN SELL PT	SELL @ PRICE	SELL AMOUNT	PROFIT/LOSS

SYMBOL:_____ Exchange:_____

DATE	BUY @ PRICE	BUY AMOUNT	MIN SELL PT	SELL @ PRICE	SELL AMOUNT	PROFIT/LOSS

SYMBOL:_____ Exchange:_____

DATE	BUY @ PRICE	BUY AMOUNT	MIN SELL PT	SELL @ PRICE	SELL AMOUNT	PROFIT/LOSS

SYMBOL:_____ Exchange:_____

DATE	BUY @ PRICE	BUY AMOUNT	MIN SELL PT	SELL @ PRICE	SELL AMOUNT	PROFIT/LOSS

SYMBOL:_____ Exchange:_____

DATE	BUY @ PRICE	BUY AMOUNT	MIN SELL PT	SELL @ PRICE	SELL AMOUNT	PROFIT/LOSS

SYMBOL:_____ Exchange:_____

DATE	BUY @ PRICE	BUY AMOUNT	MIN SELL PT	SELL @ PRICE	SELL AMOUNT	PROFIT/LOSS

SYMBOL:_____ Exchange:_____

DATE	BUY @ PRICE	BUY AMOUNT	MIN SELL PT	SELL @ PRICE	SELL AMOUNT	PROFIT/LOSS

SYMBOL:_____ Exchange:_____

DATE	BUY @ PRICE	BUY AMOUNT	MIN SELL PT	SELL @ PRICE	SELL AMOUNT	PROFIT/LOSS

SYMBOL:_____ Exchange:_____

DATE	BUY @ PRICE	BUY AMOUNT	MIN SELL PT	SELL @ PRICE	SELL AMOUNT	PROFIT/LOSS

SYMBOL:_____ Exchange:_____

DATE	BUY @ PRICE	BUY AMOUNT	MIN SELL PT	SELL @ PRICE	SELL AMOUNT	PROFIT/LOSS

SYMBOL:_____ Exchange:_____

DATE	BUY @ PRICE	BUY AMOUNT	MIN SELL PT	SELL @ PRICE	SELL AMOUNT	PROFIT/LOSS

SYMBOL:_____ Exchange:_____

DATE	BUY @ PRICE	BUY AMOUNT	MIN SELL PT	SELL @ PRICE	SELL AMOUNT	PROFIT/LOSS

SYMBOL:_____ Exchange:_____

DATE	BUY @ PRICE	BUY AMOUNT	MIN SELL PT	SELL @ PRICE	SELL AMOUNT	PROFIT/LOSS

SYMBOL:_____ Exchange:_____

DATE	BUY @ PRICE	BUY AMOUNT	MIN SELL PT	SELL @ PRICE	SELL AMOUNT	PROFIT/LOSS

SYMBOL:_____ Exchange:_____

DATE	BUY @ PRICE	BUY AMOUNT	MIN SELL PT	SELL @ PRICE	SELL AMOUNT	PROFIT/LOSS

SYMBOL:_____ Exchange:_____

DATE	BUY @ PRICE	BUY AMOUNT	MIN SELL PT	SELL @ PRICE	SELL AMOUNT	PROFIT/LOSS

SYMBOL:_____ Exchange:_____

DATE	BUY @ PRICE	BUY AMOUNT	MIN SELL PT	SELL @ PRICE	SELL AMOUNT	PROFIT/LOSS

SYMBOL:_____ Exchange:_____

DATE	BUY @ PRICE	BUY AMOUNT	MIN SELL PT	SELL @ PRICE	SELL AMOUNT	PROFIT/LOSS

SYMBOL:_____ Exchange:_____

DATE	BUY @ PRICE	BUY AMOUNT	MIN SELL PT	SELL @ PRICE	SELL AMOUNT	PROFIT/LOSS

SYMBOL:_____ Exchange:_____

DATE	BUY @ PRICE	BUY AMOUNT	MIN SELL PT	SELL @ PRICE	SELL AMOUNT	PROFIT/LOSS

SYMBOL:_____ Exchange:_____

DATE	BUY @ PRICE	BUY AMOUNT	MIN SELL PT	SELL @ PRICE	SELL AMOUNT	PROFIT/LOSS

SYMBOL:_____ Exchange:_____

DATE	BUY @ PRICE	BUY AMOUNT	MIN SELL PT	SELL @ PRICE	SELL AMOUNT	PROFIT/LOSS

SYMBOL:_____ Exchange:_____

DATE	BUY @ PRICE	BUY AMOUNT	MIN SELL PT	SELL @ PRICE	SELL AMOUNT	PROFIT/LOSS

SYMBOL:_____ Exchange:_____

DATE	BUY @ PRICE	BUY AMOUNT	MIN SELL PT	SELL @ PRICE	SELL AMOUNT	PROFIT/LOSS

SYMBOL:_____ Exchange:_____

DATE	BUY @ PRICE	BUY AMOUNT	MIN SELL PT	SELL @ PRICE	SELL AMOUNT	PROFIT/LOSS

SYMBOL:_____ Exchange:_____

DATE	BUY @ PRICE	BUY AMOUNT	MIN SELL PT	SELL @ PRICE	SELL AMOUNT	PROFIT/LOSS

SYMBOL:_____ Exchange:_____

DATE	BUY @ PRICE	BUY AMOUNT	MIN SELL PT	SELL @ PRICE	SELL AMOUNT	PROFIT/LOSS

SYMBOL:_____ Exchange:_____

DATE	BUY @ PRICE	BUY AMOUNT	MIN SELL PT	SELL @ PRICE	SELL AMOUNT	PROFIT/LOSS

SYMBOL:_____ Exchange:_____

DATE	BUY @ PRICE	BUY AMOUNT	MIN SELL PT	SELL @ PRICE	SELL AMOUNT	PROFIT/LOSS

SYMBOL:_____ Exchange:_____

DATE	BUY @ PRICE	BUY AMOUNT	MIN SELL PT	SELL @ PRICE	SELL AMOUNT	PROFIT/LOSS

SYMBOL:_____ Exchange:_____

DATE	BUY @ PRICE	BUY AMOUNT	MIN SELL PT	SELL @ PRICE	SELL AMOUNT	PROFIT/LOSS

SYMBOL:_____ Exchange:_____

DATE	BUY @ PRICE	BUY AMOUNT	MIN SELL PT	SELL @ PRICE	SELL AMOUNT	PROFIT/LOSS

SYMBOL:_____ Exchange:_____

DATE	BUY @ PRICE	BUY AMOUNT	MIN SELL PT	SELL @ PRICE	SELL AMOUNT	PROFIT/LOSS

SYMBOL:_____ Exchange:_____

DATE	BUY @ PRICE	BUY AMOUNT	MIN SELL PT	SELL @ PRICE	SELL AMOUNT	PROFIT/LOSS

SYMBOL:_____ Exchange:_____

DATE	BUY @ PRICE	BUY AMOUNT	MIN SELL PT	SELL @ PRICE	SELL AMOUNT	PROFIT/LOSS

SYMBOL:_____ Exchange:_____

DATE	BUY @ PRICE	BUY AMOUNT	MIN SELL PT	SELL @ PRICE	SELL AMOUNT	PROFIT/LOSS

SYMBOL:_____ Exchange:_____

DATE	BUY @ PRICE	BUY AMOUNT	MIN SELL PT	SELL @ PRICE	SELL AMOUNT	PROFIT/LOSS

SYMBOL:_____ Exchange:_____

DATE	BUY @ PRICE	BUY AMOUNT	MIN SELL PT	SELL @ PRICE	SELL AMOUNT	PROFIT/LOSS

SYMBOL:_____ Exchange:_____

DATE	BUY @ PRICE	BUY AMOUNT	MIN SELL PT	SELL @ PRICE	SELL AMOUNT	PROFIT/LOSS

SYMBOL:_____ Exchange:_____

DATE	BUY @ PRICE	BUY AMOUNT	MIN SELL PT	SELL @ PRICE	SELL AMOUNT	PROFIT/LOSS

SYMBOL:_____ Exchange:_____

DATE	BUY @ PRICE	BUY AMOUNT	MIN SELL PT	SELL @ PRICE	SELL AMOUNT	PROFIT/LOSS

SYMBOL:_____ Exchange:_____

DATE	BUY @ PRICE	BUY AMOUNT	MIN SELL PT	SELL @ PRICE	SELL AMOUNT	PROFIT/LOSS

SYMBOL:_____ Exchange:_____

DATE	BUY @ PRICE	BUY AMOUNT	MIN SELL PT	SELL @ PRICE	SELL AMOUNT	PROFIT/LOSS

SYMBOL:_____ Exchange:_____

DATE	BUY @ PRICE	BUY AMOUNT	MIN SELL PT	SELL @ PRICE	SELL AMOUNT	PROFIT/LOSS

SYMBOL:_____ Exchange:_____

DATE	BUY @ PRICE	BUY AMOUNT	MIN SELL PT	SELL @ PRICE	SELL AMOUNT	PROFIT/LOSS

SYMBOL:_____ Exchange:_____

DATE	BUY @ PRICE	BUY AMOUNT	MIN SELL PT	SELL @ PRICE	SELL AMOUNT	PROFIT/LOSS

SYMBOL:_____ Exchange:_____

DATE	BUY @ PRICE	BUY AMOUNT	MIN SELL PT	SELL @ PRICE	SELL AMOUNT	PROFIT/LOSS

SYMBOL:_____ Exchange:_____

DATE	BUY @ PRICE	BUY AMOUNT	MIN SELL PT	SELL @ PRICE	SELL AMOUNT	PROFIT/LOSS

SYMBOL:_____ Exchange:_____

DATE	BUY @ PRICE	BUY AMOUNT	MIN SELL PT	SELL @ PRICE	SELL AMOUNT	PROFIT/LOSS

SYMBOL:_____ Exchange:_____

DATE	BUY @ PRICE	BUY AMOUNT	MIN SELL PT	SELL @ PRICE	SELL AMOUNT	PROFIT/LOSS

SYMBOL:_____ Exchange:_____

DATE	BUY @ PRICE	BUY AMOUNT	MIN SELL PT	SELL @ PRICE	SELL AMOUNT	PROFIT/LOSS

SYMBOL:_____ Exchange:_____

DATE	BUY @ PRICE	BUY AMOUNT	MIN SELL PT	SELL @ PRICE	SELL AMOUNT	PROFIT/LOSS

SYMBOL:_____ Exchange:_____

DATE	BUY @ PRICE	BUY AMOUNT	MIN SELL PT	SELL @ PRICE	SELL AMOUNT	PROFIT/LOSS

SYMBOL:_____ Exchange:_____

DATE	BUY @ PRICE	BUY AMOUNT	MIN SELL PT	SELL @ PRICE	SELL AMOUNT	PROFIT/LOSS

SYMBOL:_____ Exchange:_____

DATE	BUY @ PRICE	BUY AMOUNT	MIN SELL PT	SELL @ PRICE	SELL AMOUNT	PROFIT/LOSS

SYMBOL:_____ Exchange:_____

DATE	BUY @ PRICE	BUY AMOUNT	MIN SELL PT	SELL @ PRICE	SELL AMOUNT	PROFIT/LOSS

SYMBOL:_____ Exchange:_____

DATE	BUY @ PRICE	BUY AMOUNT	MIN SELL PT	SELL @ PRICE	SELL AMOUNT	PROFIT/LOSS

SYMBOL:_____ Exchange:_____

DATE	BUY @ PRICE	BUY AMOUNT	MIN SELL PT	SELL @ PRICE	SELL AMOUNT	PROFIT/LOSS

SYMBOL:_____ Exchange:_____

DATE	BUY @ PRICE	BUY AMOUNT	MIN SELL PT	SELL @ PRICE	SELL AMOUNT	PROFIT/LOSS

SYMBOL:_____ Exchange:_____

DATE	BUY @ PRICE	BUY AMOUNT	MIN SELL PT	SELL @ PRICE	SELL AMOUNT	PROFIT/LOSS

SYMBOL:_____ Exchange:_____

DATE	BUY @ PRICE	BUY AMOUNT	MIN SELL PT	SELL @ PRICE	SELL AMOUNT	PROFIT/LOSS

SYMBOL:_____ Exchange:_____

DATE	BUY @ PRICE	BUY AMOUNT	MIN SELL PT	SELL @ PRICE	SELL AMOUNT	PROFIT/LOSS

SYMBOL:_____ Exchange:_____

DATE	BUY @ PRICE	BUY AMOUNT	MIN SELL PT	SELL @ PRICE	SELL AMOUNT	PROFIT/LOSS

SYMBOL:_____ Exchange:_____

DATE	BUY @ PRICE	BUY AMOUNT	MIN SELL PT	SELL @ PRICE	SELL AMOUNT	PROFIT/LOSS

SYMBOL:_____ Exchange:_____

DATE	BUY @ PRICE	BUY AMOUNT	MIN SELL PT	SELL @ PRICE	SELL AMOUNT	PROFIT/LOSS

SYMBOL:_____ Exchange:_____

DATE	BUY @ PRICE	BUY AMOUNT	MIN SELL PT	SELL @ PRICE	SELL AMOUNT	PROFIT/LOSS

SYMBOL:_____ Exchange:_____

DATE	BUY @ PRICE	BUY AMOUNT	MIN SELL PT	SELL @ PRICE	SELL AMOUNT	PROFIT/LOSS

SYMBOL:_____ Exchange:_____

DATE	BUY @ PRICE	BUY AMOUNT	MIN SELL PT	SELL @ PRICE	SELL AMOUNT	PROFIT/LOSS

SYMBOL:_____ Exchange:_____

DATE	BUY @ PRICE	BUY AMOUNT	MIN SELL PT	SELL @ PRICE	SELL AMOUNT	PROFIT/LOSS

SYMBOL:_____ Exchange:_____

DATE	BUY @ PRICE	BUY AMOUNT	MIN SELL PT	SELL @ PRICE	SELL AMOUNT	PROFIT/LOSS

SYMBOL:_____ Exchange:_____

DATE	BUY @ PRICE	BUY AMOUNT	MIN SELL PT	SELL @ PRICE	SELL AMOUNT	PROFIT/LOSS

SYMBOL:_____ Exchange:_____

DATE	BUY @ PRICE	BUY AMOUNT	MIN SELL PT	SELL @ PRICE	SELL AMOUNT	PROFIT/LOSS

SYMBOL:_____ Exchange:_____

DATE	BUY @ PRICE	BUY AMOUNT	MIN SELL PT	SELL @ PRICE	SELL AMOUNT	PROFIT/LOSS

SYMBOL:_____ Exchange:_____

DATE	BUY @ PRICE	BUY AMOUNT	MIN SELL PT	SELL @ PRICE	SELL AMOUNT	PROFIT/LOSS

SYMBOL:_____ Exchange:_____

DATE	BUY @ PRICE	BUY AMOUNT	MIN SELL PT	SELL @ PRICE	SELL AMOUNT	PROFIT/LOSS

SYMBOL:_____ Exchange:_____

DATE	BUY @ PRICE	BUY AMOUNT	MIN SELL PT	SELL @ PRICE	SELL AMOUNT	PROFIT/LOSS

SYMBOL:_____ Exchange:_____

DATE	BUY @ PRICE	BUY AMOUNT	MIN SELL PT	SELL @ PRICE	SELL AMOUNT	PROFIT/LOSS

SYMBOL:_____ Exchange:_____

DATE	BUY @ PRICE	BUY AMOUNT	MIN SELL PT	SELL @ PRICE	SELL AMOUNT	PROFIT/LOSS

SYMBOL:_____ Exchange:_____

DATE	BUY @ PRICE	BUY AMOUNT	MIN SELL PT	SELL @ PRICE	SELL AMOUNT	PROFIT/LOSS

SYMBOL:_____ Exchange:_____

DATE	BUY @ PRICE	BUY AMOUNT	MIN SELL PT	SELL @ PRICE	SELL AMOUNT	PROFIT/LOSS

SYMBOL:_____ Exchange:_____

DATE	BUY @ PRICE	BUY AMOUNT	MIN SELL PT	SELL @ PRICE	SELL AMOUNT	PROFIT/LOSS

SYMBOL:_____ Exchange:_____

DATE	BUY @ PRICE	BUY AMOUNT	MIN SELL PT	SELL @ PRICE	SELL AMOUNT	PROFIT/LOSS

SYMBOL:_____ Exchange:_____

DATE	BUY @ PRICE	BUY AMOUNT	MIN SELL PT	SELL @ PRICE	SELL AMOUNT	PROFIT/LOSS

SYMBOL:_____ Exchange:_____

DATE	BUY @ PRICE	BUY AMOUNT	MIN SELL PT	SELL @ PRICE	SELL AMOUNT	PROFIT/LOSS

SYMBOL:_____ Exchange:_____

DATE	BUY @ PRICE	BUY AMOUNT	MIN SELL PT	SELL @ PRICE	SELL AMOUNT	PROFIT/LOSS

SYMBOL:_____ Exchange:_____

DATE	BUY @ PRICE	BUY AMOUNT	MIN SELL PT	SELL @ PRICE	SELL AMOUNT	PROFIT/LOSS

SYMBOL:_____ Exchange:_____

DATE	BUY @ PRICE	BUY AMOUNT	MIN SELL PT	SELL @ PRICE	SELL AMOUNT	PROFIT/LOSS

SYMBOL:_____ Exchange:_____

DATE	BUY @ PRICE	BUY AMOUNT	MIN SELL PT	SELL @ PRICE	SELL AMOUNT	PROFIT/LOSS

SYMBOL:_____ Exchange:_____

DATE	BUY @ PRICE	BUY AMOUNT	MIN SELL PT	SELL @ PRICE	SELL AMOUNT	PROFIT/LOSS

SYMBOL:_____ Exchange:_____

DATE	BUY @ PRICE	BUY AMOUNT	MIN SELL PT	SELL @ PRICE	SELL AMOUNT	PROFIT/LOSS

SYMBOL:_____ Exchange:_____

DATE	BUY @ PRICE	BUY AMOUNT	MIN SELL PT	SELL @ PRICE	SELL AMOUNT	PROFIT/LOSS

SYMBOL:_____ Exchange:_____

DATE	BUY @ PRICE	BUY AMOUNT	MIN SELL PT	SELL @ PRICE	SELL AMOUNT	PROFIT/LOSS

SYMBOL:_____ Exchange:_____

DATE	BUY @ PRICE	BUY AMOUNT	MIN SELL PT	SELL @ PRICE	SELL AMOUNT	PROFIT/LOSS

SYMBOL:_____ Exchange:_____

DATE	BUY @ PRICE	BUY AMOUNT	MIN SELL PT	SELL @ PRICE	SELL AMOUNT	PROFIT/LOSS

SYMBOL:_____ Exchange:_____

DATE	BUY @ PRICE	BUY AMOUNT	MIN SELL PT	SELL @ PRICE	SELL AMOUNT	PROFIT/LOSS

SYMBOL:_____ Exchange:_____

DATE	BUY @ PRICE	BUY AMOUNT	MIN SELL PT	SELL @ PRICE	SELL AMOUNT	PROFIT/LOSS

SYMBOL:_____ Exchange:_____

DATE	BUY @ PRICE	BUY AMOUNT	MIN SELL PT	SELL @ PRICE	SELL AMOUNT	PROFIT/LOSS

SYMBOL:_____ Exchange:_____

DATE	BUY @ PRICE	BUY AMOUNT	MIN SELL PT	SELL @ PRICE	SELL AMOUNT	PROFIT/LOSS

SYMBOL:_____ Exchange:_____

DATE	BUY @ PRICE	BUY AMOUNT	MIN SELL PT	SELL @ PRICE	SELL AMOUNT	PROFIT/LOSS

SYMBOL:_____ Exchange:_____

DATE	BUY @ PRICE	BUY AMOUNT	MIN SELL PT	SELL @ PRICE	SELL AMOUNT	PROFIT/LOSS

SYMBOL:_____ Exchange:_____

DATE	BUY @ PRICE	BUY AMOUNT	MIN SELL PT	SELL @ PRICE	SELL AMOUNT	PROFIT/LOSS

SYMBOL:_____ Exchange:_____

DATE	BUY @ PRICE	BUY AMOUNT	MIN SELL PT	SELL @ PRICE	SELL AMOUNT	PROFIT/LOSS

SYMBOL:_____ Exchange:_____

DATE	BUY @ PRICE	BUY AMOUNT	MIN SELL PT	SELL @ PRICE	SELL AMOUNT	PROFIT/LOSS

SYMBOL:_____ Exchange:_____

DATE	BUY @ PRICE	BUY AMOUNT	MIN SELL PT	SELL @ PRICE	SELL AMOUNT	PROFIT/LOSS

SYMBOL:_____ Exchange:_____

DATE	BUY @ PRICE	BUY AMOUNT	MIN SELL PT	SELL @ PRICE	SELL AMOUNT	PROFIT/LOSS

SYMBOL:_____ Exchange:_____

DATE	BUY @ PRICE	BUY AMOUNT	MIN SELL PT	SELL @ PRICE	SELL AMOUNT	PROFIT/LOSS

SYMBOL:_____ Exchange:_____

DATE	BUY @ PRICE	BUY AMOUNT	MIN SELL PT	SELL @ PRICE	SELL AMOUNT	PROFIT/LOSS

SYMBOL:_____ Exchange:_____

DATE	BUY @ PRICE	BUY AMOUNT	MIN SELL PT	SELL @ PRICE	SELL AMOUNT	PROFIT/LOSS

SYMBOL:_____ Exchange:_____

DATE	BUY @ PRICE	BUY AMOUNT	MIN SELL PT	SELL @ PRICE	SELL AMOUNT	PROFIT/LOSS

SYMBOL:_____ Exchange:_____

DATE	BUY @ PRICE	BUY AMOUNT	MIN SELL PT	SELL @ PRICE	SELL AMOUNT	PROFIT/LOSS

SYMBOL:_____ Exchange:_____

DATE	BUY @ PRICE	BUY AMOUNT	MIN SELL PT	SELL @ PRICE	SELL AMOUNT	PROFIT/LOSS

SYMBOL:_____ Exchange:_____

DATE	BUY @ PRICE	BUY AMOUNT	MIN SELL PT	SELL @ PRICE	SELL AMOUNT	PROFIT/LOSS

SYMBOL:_____ Exchange:_____

DATE	BUY @ PRICE	BUY AMOUNT	MIN SELL PT	SELL @ PRICE	SELL AMOUNT	PROFIT/LOSS

SYMBOL:_____ Exchange:_____

DATE	BUY @ PRICE	BUY AMOUNT	MIN SELL PT	SELL @ PRICE	SELL AMOUNT	PROFIT/LOSS

SYMBOL:_____ Exchange:_____

DATE	BUY @ PRICE	BUY AMOUNT	MIN SELL PT	SELL @ PRICE	SELL AMOUNT	PROFIT/LOSS

SYMBOL:_____ Exchange:_____

DATE	BUY @ PRICE	BUY AMOUNT	MIN SELL PT	SELL @ PRICE	SELL AMOUNT	PROFIT/LOSS

SYMBOL:_____ Exchange:_____

DATE	BUY @ PRICE	BUY AMOUNT	MIN SELL PT	SELL @ PRICE	SELL AMOUNT	PROFIT/LOSS

SYMBOL:_____ Exchange:_____

DATE	BUY @ PRICE	BUY AMOUNT	MIN SELL PT	SELL @ PRICE	SELL AMOUNT	PROFIT/LOSS

SYMBOL:_____ Exchange:_____

DATE	BUY @ PRICE	BUY AMOUNT	MIN SELL PT	SELL @ PRICE	SELL AMOUNT	PROFIT/LOSS

SYMBOL:_____ Exchange:_____

DATE	BUY @ PRICE	BUY AMOUNT	MIN SELL PT	SELL @ PRICE	SELL AMOUNT	PROFIT/LOSS

SYMBOL:_____ Exchange:_____

DATE	BUY @ PRICE	BUY AMOUNT	MIN SELL PT	SELL @ PRICE	SELL AMOUNT	PROFIT/LOSS

SYMBOL:_____ Exchange:_____

DATE	BUY @ PRICE	BUY AMOUNT	MIN SELL PT	SELL @ PRICE	SELL AMOUNT	PROFIT/LOSS

SYMBOL:_____ Exchange:_____

DATE	BUY @ PRICE	BUY AMOUNT	MIN SELL PT	SELL @ PRICE	SELL AMOUNT	PROFIT/LOSS

SYMBOL:_____ Exchange:_____

DATE	BUY @ PRICE	BUY AMOUNT	MIN SELL PT	SELL @ PRICE	SELL AMOUNT	PROFIT/LOSS

SYMBOL:_____ Exchange:_____

DATE	BUY @ PRICE	BUY AMOUNT	MIN SELL PT	SELL @ PRICE	SELL AMOUNT	PROFIT/LOSS

SYMBOL:_____ Exchange:_____

DATE	BUY @ PRICE	BUY AMOUNT	MIN SELL PT	SELL @ PRICE	SELL AMOUNT	PROFIT/LOSS

SYMBOL:_____ Exchange:_____

DATE	BUY @ PRICE	BUY AMOUNT	MIN SELL PT	SELL @ PRICE	SELL AMOUNT	PROFIT/LOSS

SYMBOL:_____ Exchange:_____

DATE	BUY @ PRICE	BUY AMOUNT	MIN SELL PT	SELL @ PRICE	SELL AMOUNT	PROFIT/LOSS

SYMBOL:_____ Exchange:_____

DATE	BUY @ PRICE	BUY AMOUNT	MIN SELL PT	SELL @ PRICE	SELL AMOUNT	PROFIT/LOSS

SYMBOL:_____ Exchange:_____

DATE	BUY @ PRICE	BUY AMOUNT	MIN SELL PT	SELL @ PRICE	SELL AMOUNT	PROFIT/LOSS

SYMBOL:_____ Exchange:_____

DATE	BUY @ PRICE	BUY AMOUNT	MIN SELL PT	SELL @ PRICE	SELL AMOUNT	PROFIT/LOSS

SYMBOL:_____ Exchange:_____

DATE	BUY @ PRICE	BUY AMOUNT	MIN SELL PT	SELL @ PRICE	SELL AMOUNT	PROFIT/LOSS

SYMBOL:_____ Exchange:_____

DATE	BUY @ PRICE	BUY AMOUNT	MIN SELL PT	SELL @ PRICE	SELL AMOUNT	PROFIT/LOSS

SYMBOL:_____ Exchange:_____

DATE	BUY @ PRICE	BUY AMOUNT	MIN SELL PT	SELL @ PRICE	SELL AMOUNT	PROFIT/LOSS

SYMBOL:_____ Exchange:_____

DATE	BUY @ PRICE	BUY AMOUNT	MIN SELL PT	SELL @ PRICE	SELL AMOUNT	PROFIT/LOSS

SYMBOL:_____ Exchange:_____

DATE	BUY @ PRICE	BUY AMOUNT	MIN SELL PT	SELL @ PRICE	SELL AMOUNT	PROFIT/LOSS

SYMBOL:_____ Exchange:_____

DATE	BUY @ PRICE	BUY AMOUNT	MIN SELL PT	SELL @ PRICE	SELL AMOUNT	PROFIT/LOSS

SYMBOL:_____ Exchange:_____

DATE	BUY @ PRICE	BUY AMOUNT	MIN SELL PT	SELL @ PRICE	SELL AMOUNT	PROFIT/LOSS

SYMBOL:_____ Exchange:_____

DATE	BUY @ PRICE	BUY AMOUNT	MIN SELL PT	SELL @ PRICE	SELL AMOUNT	PROFIT/LOSS

SYMBOL:_____ Exchange:_____

DATE	BUY @ PRICE	BUY AMOUNT	MIN SELL PT	SELL @ PRICE	SELL AMOUNT	PROFIT/LOSS

SYMBOL:_____ Exchange:_____

DATE	BUY @ PRICE	BUY AMOUNT	MIN SELL PT	SELL @ PRICE	SELL AMOUNT	PROFIT/LOSS

SYMBOL:_____ Exchange:_____

DATE	BUY @ PRICE	BUY AMOUNT	MIN SELL PT	SELL @ PRICE	SELL AMOUNT	PROFIT/LOSS

SYMBOL:_____ Exchange:_____

DATE	BUY @ PRICE	BUY AMOUNT	MIN SELL PT	SELL @ PRICE	SELL AMOUNT	PROFIT/LOSS

SYMBOL:_____ Exchange:_____

DATE	BUY @ PRICE	BUY AMOUNT	MIN SELL PT	SELL @ PRICE	SELL AMOUNT	PROFIT/LOSS

SYMBOL:_____ Exchange:_____

DATE	BUY @ PRICE	BUY AMOUNT	MIN SELL PT	SELL @ PRICE	SELL AMOUNT	PROFIT/LOSS

SYMBOL:_____ Exchange:_____

DATE	BUY @ PRICE	BUY AMOUNT	MIN SELL PT	SELL @ PRICE	SELL AMOUNT	PROFIT/LOSS

SYMBOL:_____ Exchange:_____

DATE	BUY @ PRICE	BUY AMOUNT	MIN SELL PT	SELL @ PRICE	SELL AMOUNT	PROFIT/LOSS

SYMBOL:_____ Exchange:_____

DATE	BUY @ PRICE	BUY AMOUNT	MIN SELL PT	SELL @ PRICE	SELL AMOUNT	PROFIT/LOSS

SYMBOL:_____ Exchange:_____

DATE	BUY @ PRICE	BUY AMOUNT	MIN SELL PT	SELL @ PRICE	SELL AMOUNT	PROFIT/LOSS

SYMBOL:_____ Exchange:_____

DATE	BUY @ PRICE	BUY AMOUNT	MIN SELL PT	SELL @ PRICE	SELL AMOUNT	PROFIT/LOSS

SYMBOL:_____ Exchange:_____

DATE	BUY @ PRICE	BUY AMOUNT	MIN SELL PT	SELL @ PRICE	SELL AMOUNT	PROFIT/LOSS

SYMBOL:_____ Exchange:_____

DATE	BUY @ PRICE	BUY AMOUNT	MIN SELL PT	SELL @ PRICE	SELL AMOUNT	PROFIT/LOSS

SYMBOL:_____ Exchange:_____

DATE	BUY @ PRICE	BUY AMOUNT	MIN SELL PT	SELL @ PRICE	SELL AMOUNT	PROFIT/LOSS

SYMBOL:_____ Exchange:_____

DATE	BUY @ PRICE	BUY AMOUNT	MIN SELL PT	SELL @ PRICE	SELL AMOUNT	PROFIT/LOSS

SYMBOL:_____ Exchange:_____

DATE	BUY @ PRICE	BUY AMOUNT	MIN SELL PT	SELL @ PRICE	SELL AMOUNT	PROFIT/LOSS

SYMBOL:_____ Exchange:_____

DATE	BUY @ PRICE	BUY AMOUNT	MIN SELL PT	SELL @ PRICE	SELL AMOUNT	PROFIT/LOSS

SYMBOL:_____ Exchange:_____

DATE	BUY @ PRICE	BUY AMOUNT	MIN SELL PT	SELL @ PRICE	SELL AMOUNT	PROFIT/LOSS

SYMBOL:_____ Exchange:_____

DATE	BUY @ PRICE	BUY AMOUNT	MIN SELL PT	SELL @ PRICE	SELL AMOUNT	PROFIT/LOSS

SYMBOL:_____ Exchange:_____

DATE	BUY @ PRICE	BUY AMOUNT	MIN SELL PT	SELL @ PRICE	SELL AMOUNT	PROFIT/LOSS

SYMBOL:_____ Exchange:_____

DATE	BUY @ PRICE	BUY AMOUNT	MIN SELL PT	SELL @ PRICE	SELL AMOUNT	PROFIT/LOSS

SYMBOL:_____ Exchange:_____

DATE	BUY @ PRICE	BUY AMOUNT	MIN SELL PT	SELL @ PRICE	SELL AMOUNT	PROFIT/LOSS

SYMBOL:_____ Exchange:_____

DATE	BUY @ PRICE	BUY AMOUNT	MIN SELL PT	SELL @ PRICE	SELL AMOUNT	PROFIT/LOSS

SYMBOL:_____ Exchange:_____

DATE	BUY @ PRICE	BUY AMOUNT	MIN SELL PT	SELL @ PRICE	SELL AMOUNT	PROFIT/LOSS

SYMBOL:_____ Exchange:_____

DATE	BUY @ PRICE	BUY AMOUNT	MIN SELL PT	SELL @ PRICE	SELL AMOUNT	PROFIT/LOSS

SYMBOL:_____ Exchange:_____

DATE	BUY @ PRICE	BUY AMOUNT	MIN SELL PT	SELL @ PRICE	SELL AMOUNT	PROFIT/LOSS

SYMBOL:_____ Exchange:_____

DATE	BUY @ PRICE	BUY AMOUNT	MIN SELL PT	SELL @ PRICE	SELL AMOUNT	PROFIT/LOSS

SYMBOL:_____ Exchange:_____

DATE	BUY @ PRICE	BUY AMOUNT	MIN SELL PT	SELL @ PRICE	SELL AMOUNT	PROFIT/LOSS

SYMBOL:_____ Exchange:_____

DATE	BUY @ PRICE	BUY AMOUNT	MIN SELL PT	SELL @ PRICE	SELL AMOUNT	PROFIT/LOSS

SYMBOL:_____ Exchange:_____

DATE	BUY @ PRICE	BUY AMOUNT	MIN SELL PT	SELL @ PRICE	SELL AMOUNT	PROFIT/LOSS

SYMBOL:_____ Exchange:_____

DATE	BUY @ PRICE	BUY AMOUNT	MIN SELL PT	SELL @ PRICE	SELL AMOUNT	PROFIT/LOSS

SYMBOL:_____ Exchange:_____

DATE	BUY @ PRICE	BUY AMOUNT	MIN SELL PT	SELL @ PRICE	SELL AMOUNT	PROFIT/LOSS

SYMBOL:_____ Exchange:_____

DATE	BUY @ PRICE	BUY AMOUNT	MIN SELL PT	SELL @ PRICE	SELL AMOUNT	PROFIT/LOSS

www.ingramcontent.com/pod-product-compliance
Lightning Source LLC
Chambersburg PA
CBHW081720220526
45468CB00008B/1914